QUEENS OF THE ANIMAL UNIVERSE

ORCA COWS
Leaders of the Pod

by Jaclyn Jaycox

PEBBLE
a capstone imprint

Published by Pebble, an imprint of Capstone
1710 Roe Crest Drive,
North Mankato, Minnesota 56003
capstonepub.com

Library of Congress Cataloging-in-Publication Data
Names: Jaycox, Jaclyn, 1983- author.
Title: Orca cows : leaders of the pod / by Jaclyn Jaycox.
Description: North Mankato, Minnesota : Pebble, [2023] | Series: Queens of the animal universe | Includes bibliographical references and index. | Audience: Ages 5-8 | Audience: Grades K-1 | Summary: "An orca mother calls out. Her baby has gotten too far away. The sound travels through the water. The young calf hears the call. It swims back toward the group. Female orcas, or cows, lead an orca pod. They raise young and help the pod find food. Take a look at orcas and the important roles cows play to ensure the pod's survival"-- Provided by publisher.
Identifiers: LCCN 2021054288 (print) | LCCN 2021054289 (ebook) | ISBN 9781666343052 (hardcover) | ISBN 9781666343113 (paperback) | ISBN 9781666343175 (pdf) | ISBN 9781666343298 (kindle edition)
Subjects: LCSH: Killer whale--Behavior--Juvenile literature. | Social hierarchy in animals--Juvenile literature. | Social behavior in animals--Juvenile literature. | Animal societies--Juvenile literature.
Classification: LCC QL737.C432 J395 2023 (print) | LCC QL737.C432 (ebook)
| DDC 599.53/615--dc23/eng/20211122
LC record available at https://lccn.loc.gov/2021054288
LC ebook record available at https://lccn.loc.gov/2021054289

Editorial Credits
Editor: Carrie Sheely; Designer: Bobbie Nuytten; Media Researcher: Morgan Walters; Production Specialist: Polly Fisher

All internet sites appearing in back matter were available and accurate when this book was sent to press.

Table of Contents

Words in **bold** are in the glossary.

The Mighty Female

More than 5,000 kinds of **mammals** live on Earth. Of these, 76 kinds have group leaders. A male is usually the leader. But not always! Some animals have females in charge. These animal queens are key to the survival of their families. Let's learn more about female orcas!

Orcas live together in groups led by females.

Meet the Orca

Like all mammals, orcas breathe air through lungs. Young orcas drink milk from their mothers.

Orcas are sometimes called killer whales. But they aren't whales. They are a kind of dolphin. Female orcas are called cows. Males are called bulls.

Orcas swim in cold water near Norway.

Orca Range

Arctic Ocean

Europe

Asia

North America

Atlantic Ocean

Africa

Pacific Ocean

Pacific Ocean

South America

Indian Ocean

Australia

Southern Ocean

where orcas live

Orcas are **marine** animals. These animals live in water. Orcas are found in every ocean. Some live near shore. Others live far away from shore. They can be found in icy waters. They live in warm waters too.

Orcas are meat eaters. They are top ocean **predators**. No other animals hunt grown-up orcas.

Orcas eat more than 140 different kinds of **prey**. They eat fish, squid, and seals. They eat penguins and whales. Orcas hunt walruses and sharks. They even leap from the water to catch seabirds!

An orca snatches a sea lion.

The main **diet** of orcas depends on where they live. In some places, they eat mostly fish. In others, they eat mostly sea mammals.

An orca catches a penguin.

Orca Bodies

Orcas are big animals. They can grow up to 32 feet (10 meters) long. Males grow a little bigger than females.

Orcas are built for life in water. They have a long dorsal fin on their backs. This fin helps keep orcas upright. Two flippers help orcas steer. Orcas also have strong tails that push them quickly through the water.

Orcas are one of the fastest sea mammals. They can swim up to 30 miles (48 kilometers) per hour.

An orca's dorsal fin can be up to 6 feet (1.8 m) tall.

A black dorsal fin appears above the water. Whoosh! A spray of water shoots into the air. Orcas have a blowhole on top of their heads. They use the blowhole to breathe. They swim toward the surface. Just before reaching it, they breathe out. Water above the blowhole sprays up. Then they breathe in at the surface.

Orcas have black backs. Their stomachs are white. This coloring helps them blend in with their surroundings. From below, they look like sunlight. From above, they look like the dark water. It can be hard for prey to see orcas coming.

Orcas have between 40 and 56 cone-shaped teeth. They use them to catch prey. Their teeth also help them bite and tear food.

An orca's teeth can be up to 4 inches (10 centimeters) long.

Orca Families

Orcas live in family groups called **pods**. Most pods have fewer than 50 orcas. But some pods have more than 100. Most orcas stay in the same pod their whole lives.

Can you be as loud as a jet plane engine? Orcas can! They use clicks, whistles, and calls to **communicate**. Each pod has its own special calls. In deep, dark water it's hard for orcas to see. Sound is the best way to keep track of their family.

As orcas go into dark ocean waters, they keep track of where their family members are located.

Wise Leaders

A group of orcas cuts through the water. A mighty female is at the front. The hungry pod members follow behind. She's leading them to a new hunting area. Food has become hard to find. But not to worry! Their wise leader knows just where to go. Their bellies will soon be full.

Females lead pods as they travel.

Many animals die when they can't have young anymore. But not orca cows. Females stop having babies at about 40 years old. They then live much longer. Some live up to 90 years!

Over time, these older cows become leaders of the pod. They learn a lot during their long lives, such as where to find food. They pass their knowledge on to their families. Male orcas live only to about 50 years.

Orcas get to know other members of their pod well throughout their long lives. They play, hunt, and rest together.

Female orcas can have babies by the time they are around 10 years old. They are pregnant for about 17 months. They give birth to one baby at a time.

Baby orcas are called calves. The first year, they depend on their mothers for milk. It is their only food source. Calves feed often. They must drink as their mother swims!

A mother orca swims with her calf near California.

Males do not help raise the young. As calves grow, mothers teach them how to hunt as part of a group. Mothers also teach calves how to communicate in the pod.

Mothers teach calves different ways to hunt. For example, mothers may teach their calves to spy-hop. To do this, they stick their heads out of the water. Scientists think orcas do this to see prey near the surface.

Mothers usually care for their calves for about two years. Then the calves are ready to live without help.

Orcas spy-hopping

Working Together

Female orcas have tough jobs. But they don't do it alone! They help one another. Older females no longer have their own young to feed. Instead, they share it with the calves. This gives them a better chance at survival.

Orcas hunt together and share their food.

Other animals attack calves. Adult females work together to keep calves safe. They form a circle around the young. The calves stay in the middle. It keeps them protected.

Adult female orcas work together to keep calves safe.

Females also "babysit" for one another. They take turns keeping an eye on younger orcas.

Female orcas are great leaders. They teach their young. They share food. Their work helps their pod survive.

An orca pod travels near a coast.

Amazing Orca Facts

Orcas have a thick layer of fat called blubber under their skin. It keeps them warm in icy waters.

Orcas sleep with one eye open.

Orcas can hear their pods from miles away.

Adult orcas can eat 500 pounds (227 kilograms) of food a day.

Orcas have no sense of smell. They find food by sound or sight.

Orcas sometimes jump onto land or ice to catch seals.

Orcas are the largest members of the dolphin family.

The world's oldest known orca lived to be more than 100 years old. Scientists called her Granny.

Glossary

communicate (kuh-MYOO-nuh-kate)—to share information

diet (DY-uht)—what is usually eaten

mammal (MAM-uhl)—a warm–blooded animal that breathes air; mammals have hair or fur; female mammals feed milk to their young

marine (muh-REEN)—to do with water

pod (POD)—a group of orcas

predator (PRED-uh-tur)—an animal that hunts other animals for food

prey (PRAY)—an animal hunted by another animal for food

Read More

Jaycox, Jaclyn. *Killer Whales Are Awesome*. North Mankato, MN: Capstone, 2020.

Rose, Rachel. *Orca*. Minneapolis: Bearport Publishing Company, 2021.

Swanson, Jennifer. *Absolute Expert: Dolphins*. Washington, D.C.: National Geographic, 2018.

Internet Sites

Active Wild: Killer Whale Facts
activewild.com/killer-whale-facts-for-kids

Kiddle: Killer Whale Facts for Kids
kids.kiddle.co/Killer_whale

PBS: Killer Whale Fact Sheet
pbs.org/wnet/nature/blog/killer-whale-fact-sheet

Index

Author Biography

Behind the Lens Photography

Jaclyn Jaycox is a children's book author and editor. When she's not writing, she loves reading and spending time with her family. She lives in southern Minnesota with her husband, two kids, and a spunky goldendoodle.